Then and now

All the animals in this picture are reptiles. The big, fierce one died out long, long ago. Today's reptiles, such as lizards and snakes, are very different from those of the past.

Many present-day things were different in the past. Can you think of examples?

My hat

You need

newspapers

scissors

sticky tape

Now . . .

Many women wore hats like this about 500 years ago.
Try to make one from a single piece of newspaper.

Many men wore this kind of hat about 100 years ago.
Make one like it from two pieces of newspaper.
Find out what these hats were called.

Invent a hat that might be worn 100 years from now.

What was it like?

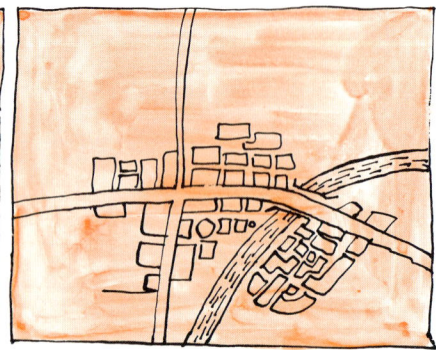

Now . . .
Look at these maps.
They show the same place
as it is now,
as it was 100 years ago,
as it was 200 years ago.
Can you say which is which?
Draw a map to show what you think it will look like a
100 years from now.

Model fossils

You need

empty shell   'Plasticine'   jam jar

'Vaseline'
strip of cardboard
plaster of Paris
tablespoon

water

Now . . .
Fossils are the remains of animals and plants
which died millions of years ago.
You needn't wait that long.
Just follow the pictures.

Fruit forms

You need
apple with stalk
kitchen knife
plate

Now . . .
Cut the apple in half.
Look for skin, flesh, core, and seeds.

Look at these drawings.
One flower makes an apple. One makes a tomato.
Which is which? How could you find out?
What kind of flowers make strawberries?

Past and present things

Use books to find out what to put in the empty boxes.
Make boxes to show past and present bicycles.
past and present dresses.

Look at churches.
Look for differences in things that grow.
Why not make a book of past and present things?

Before and after

What do you think changed this stream from a tiny trickle to a gushing torrent?

Unbalancing

You need 
birthday-cake candle
ruler 
matches 
pencil with flat sides

Now . . .
Fix the candle at one end of the ruler.
Balance the ruler across the pencil.
Light the candle.
What happens as the candle burns away?
Invent a timer using this idea.

Two in one

You need
card about 10 cm square
crayons

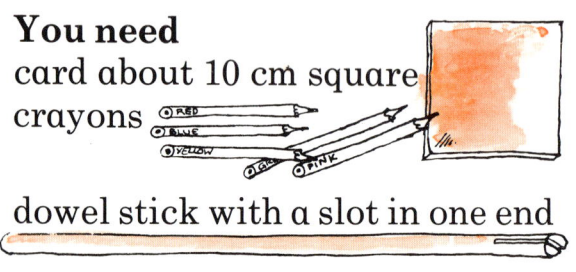

dowel stick with a slot in one end

Now . . .
Draw a big goal on the card.
Turn the card over.
Draw a small football in the middle.
Fix the card in the slot in the stick.
Roll the stick between your hands.
What happens to the ball? Why?

Make cards with different pictures.

Sweet bread

You need
bread

Now . . .
Chew a bit of bread for a long time.
Does it get sweeter? Why?
Find out what happens to bread when you eat it.

Comic cuts

You need
comic
scissors

Now . . .
Cut up a page of a comic into separate pictures.
Mix them up.
Ask friends to put the pictures in order.
Can they do it?

All change

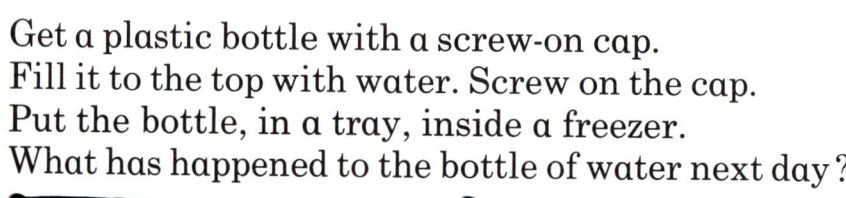

Watch how clouds change their shapes.
Look for shapes like animals, faces, or old sailing ships.
Write a poem about clouds.

Get a plastic bottle with a screw-on cap.
Fill it to the top with water. Screw on the cap.
Put the bottle, in a tray, inside a freezer.
What has happened to the bottle of water next day?

Keep a slice of bread damp in a saucer.
In a few days things start growing on the bread.
They are called moulds.
Look at them through a hand-lens.
Where do they come from?

Keep a jar of milk in a warm place.
Make a day by day record of any changes you notice.
Notice its colour, smell, and any other changes.
Look up the meaning of 'curds and whey'.

On and on

Would you like to be in the go-kart
or on the roller skates? How many ways do we know
of getting about on wheels?
Make a list.

Easier work

You need
pencils
marbles
heavy book

Now . . .
Push the book along the floor.
Now push it over your pencils.
over your marbles.
Which way is easiest?

Roll a ball

You need
narrow-gauge toy railway track
matchboxes
ping-pong ball
tennis ball
rug or strip of carpet
tape-measure

Now . . .
Slope the track using one matchbox.
Roll the ping-pong ball down the slope.
How far does it go along the carpet?
How far does it go off a 2-box slope?
a 3-box slope?
a 4-box slope?

Draw a graph.
Now do the same with the tennis ball.
What do you notice?

Mystery tins

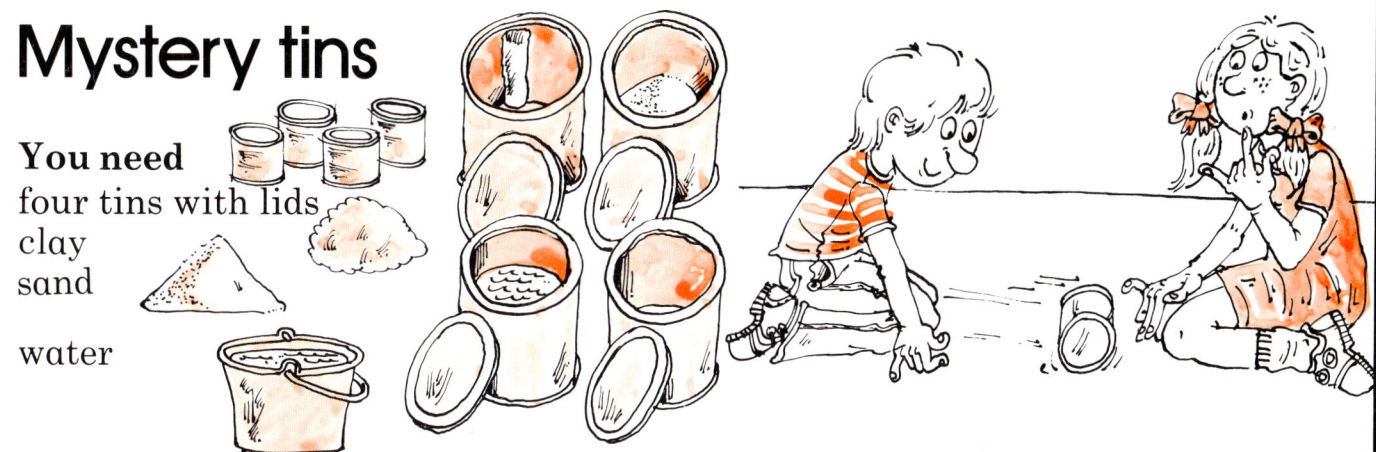

You need
four tins with lids
clay
sand

water

Now . . .
Stick a lump of clay on the side of one tin.
Half fill another tin with sand.
Half fill another tin with water.
Leave the last one empty.

Work on the floor.
Get a friend to say what the tins contain
by the way they roll!

Danger man

You need
modelling clay
metal toy car

big book

Now . . .
Make a man out of clay.
Stick him on top of the car.
Crash the car into the book.
What happens to the man if the car crashes fast?
Draw a crashing car with the driver
wearing a safety-belt.
not wearing a safety-belt.

Fun and games

How many games can you think of
which are played with a ball?
Football, netball, cricket, tennis . . .
can you go on?
Make a list.
Collect a ball, or a picture of one, for every game.
Make a card for each ball saying how big it is,
how heavy it is,
what it's made of.
Could you play cricket with a ping-pong ball?
Could you play ping-pong with a cricket ball?
Write a funny story or poem about a game played with
the wrong kind of ball.

Yes and no

How many ways can you find of crossing all the bridges without going over any twice?

Colour me happy

You need
crayons

Now . . .
Make lists of happy colours,
               sad colours,
               cold colours,
               warm colours.
Have you any cold, happy colours?
               sad, warm colours?
Draw a picture in happy colours.

Human weighing machine

You need
pebbles

Now . . .
Imagine your hand is a weighing machine.
Line up the pebbles in order of their weights.
Put the lightest first and the heaviest last

Mix up the pebbles again.
Now do the sorting with your eyes closed!
Open your eyes. What do you find?

A B C

You need
Your alphabet

ABCDEFG
HIJKLMNO
PQRSTUVW
XYZ

Now . . .
Here's a riddle.
When do mice go after cats?
            carts go before horses?
            chickens come before eggs?
When they are in alphabetical order!
Put these jumbled words in alphabetical order and find
the hidden messages:
doughnuts buys Friday every cream Aunty.
Margaret's over heavens Lady just nephew I've knocked
Good.
urchins Police rowdy quieten train soccer.
yellow X-ray won't zebras Vets.

Attractive tests

You need

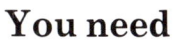

plastic

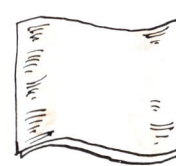
paper

glass

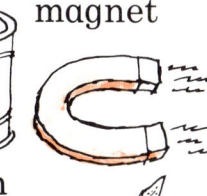
a tin

magnet

wood

cork   coal

iron

Now . . .
Make lists of things that stick to your magnet.
                that do not stick to your magnet.

Call your lists: will attract   won't attract

Find other things that stick to your magnet.

Invent an insect

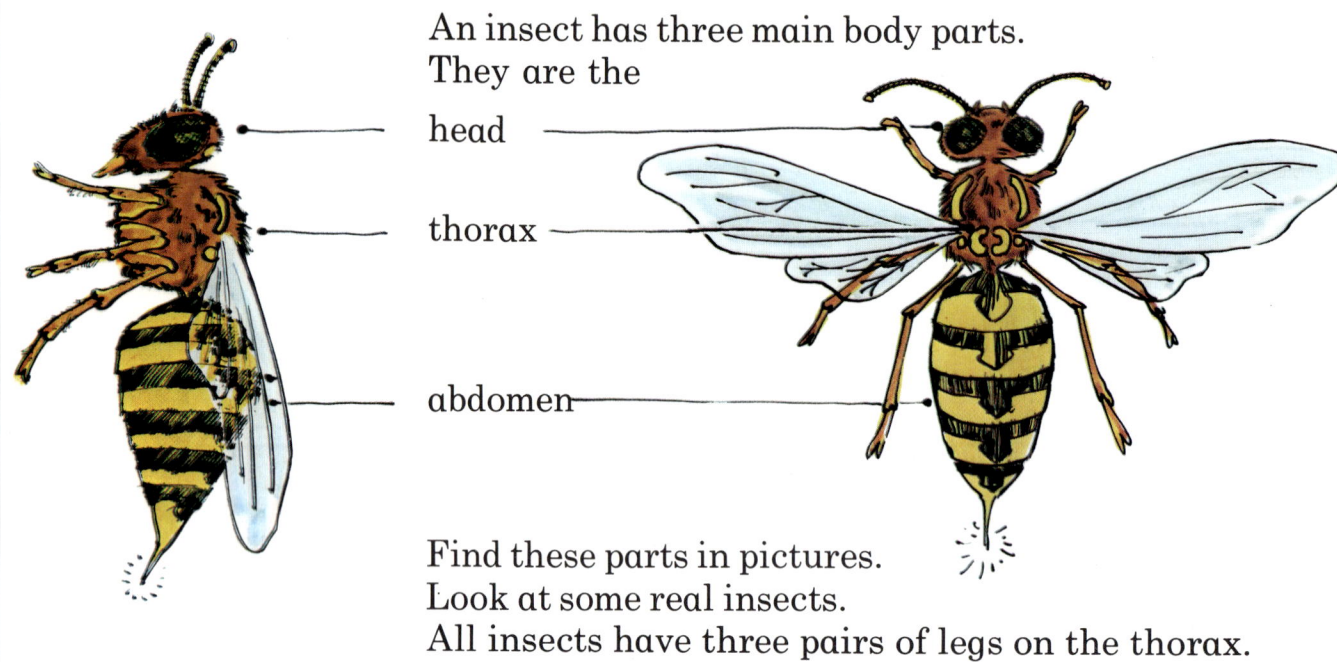

An insect has three main body parts.
They are the

head

thorax

abdomen

Find these parts in pictures.
Look at some real insects.
All insects have three pairs of legs on the thorax.
Many have two pairs of wings on the thorax.
Do they all have one pair of feelers on the head?

Draw some imaginary insects.
Make them funny
        strange
        frightening
        beautiful
Draw a big picture of the best insect you invent.
It must obey the rules!
Show your drawing in A Class Zoo of Imaginary Insects.

Well known, less known

Here are two pictures of the same beach.
See how different they are.
Lots of well known things change when something
happens to them. Think of some.

Burning fabrics

You need
tweezers
candle
matches
pieces of wool, cotton, nylon
metal spoon
scissors

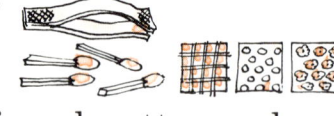

Now . . .
Cut out three small squares of wool, cotton and nylon.
Make a chart.
Hold your square of wool in tweezers
and burn it.
Collect the burnt wool in the spoon.
Describe it in your chart.
Do the same for cotton and nylon.
How have the fabrics changed?

fabric	what like after
Wool	
Cotton	
nylon	

Changing seeds

You need
bird-seed   yoghurt pots

seed compost
sticky tape

Now . . .
Spread the seed on a table.
Choose the biggest seed and
stick it on the outside of a yoghurt pot.
Put compost in the pot and
plant three seeds of the same kind.
Do the same for a different kind of seed
in another yoghurt pot.
When the seeds grow, how will they change?
Draw what you think each plant will look like.
Keep the seeds damp.

Wait and see if you were right.

Spoons and bells

You need
small and large metal spoon
string

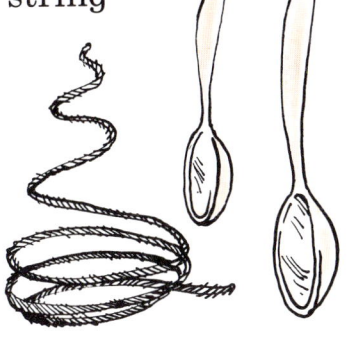

Now . . .
Tie the large spoon like this:
Swing it against a table.
What do you hear?

Now press the string to your ears like this:
Swing the spoon against the table again.
What does it sound like this time?
What happens with the small spoon?

Black eyes

You need
piece of blotting paper
black 'Pentel' pen

jam jar   water

needle   wool

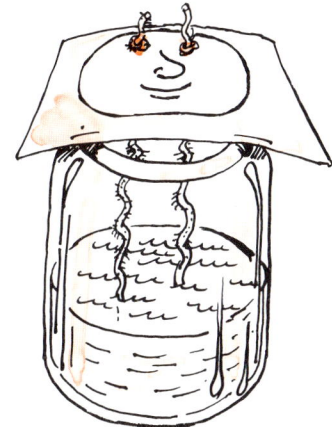

Now . . .
Draw a face on blotting paper
with the felt-tip pen.
Thread wool through each black eye.
Wet the wool.
Put the face over a jam jar of water.
Wait a few minutes.
What happens to the face?

Identikits

The police use identikits
to find missing people.
They make pictures of faces
from different
    head shapes
    eyes
    noses
    mouths
    hair

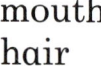

Now, imagine someone has lost a dog.
They say it has
a labrador's body
a greyhound's head
a spaniel's ears
an alsatian's tail
and an Irish-setter's legs!
Look at books about dogs.
Find pictures of the different parts.
Draw them on paper or card
and cut them out.
Make an identikit picture
to help find the dog.

Round and round

How many things go round and round in this fairground?

Meals on wheels

You need
food mixer   felt-tip pen

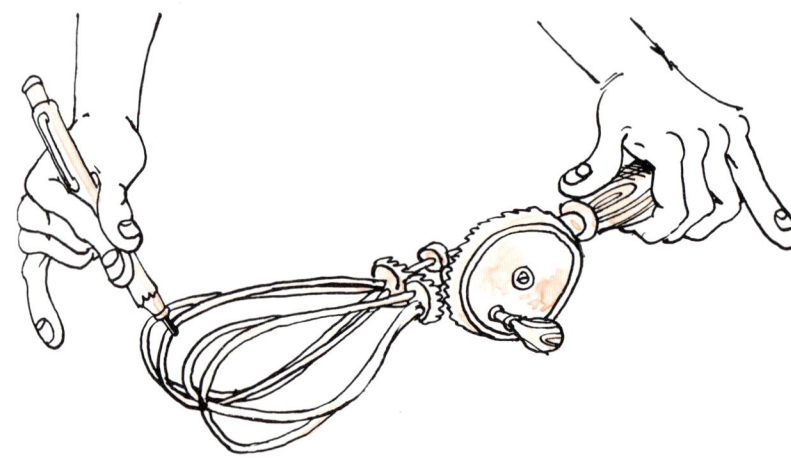

Now . . .
Mark a part of each 'mixer' with your felt-tip pen.
Turn the handle.
Watch the mixers spin.
Which turns faster, the handle or the mixers?
Do both mixers turn the same number of times?
                          in the same direction?
When the handle turns once,
how often does each mixer turn?

Compass points

You need
matchbox
toy compass
bowl of water

Now . . .
Turn the compass until its pointer is next to N.
Which part of the room is North?
Pretend the matchbox is a boat.
Put the compass on board.
Stir the water in the bowl.
Watch the compass.
How would a sailor know which way he was sailing?

Roundabout

You need
a friend

Now . . .
Spin round 3 times.
Then try walking straight towards your friend.
What happens?

Rest for a bit.
Now spin round 3 times the other way.
Try walking straight towards your friend again.
What happens this time?

Reels and bands

You need
cotton reels
nails
hammer
wooden board

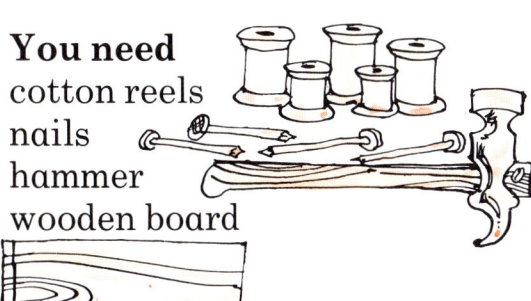

rubber bands

Now . . .
Nail the cotton reels to the board.
Join two different-size reels with a rubber band.
Turn one reel.

Does the other one turn too?
Do they both turn at the same speed?
Find out.
Try other ways of joining the reels and bands.
Can you make two reels turn in opposite directions?

Patterns

You need
three 10 × 15 cm mirrors

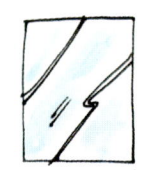

modelling clay

Use modelling clay to fix together three small mirrors.
Make the mirrors face inwards.

Stand your mirrors on white paper.
You have made a kaleidoscope!

Things to put inside your kaleidoscope:

coloured beads
toy soldiers
flowers or leaves
a woodlouse (be gentle!)

Stick a bit of tissue paper over a bicycle lamp.
Stand your kaleidoscope on the lamp, like this:

The lamp lights up the patterns inside.
Copy your best patterns.
Can you make your patterns turn?

Regular and irregular

One group looks regular.
The other group looks irregular.
Look for regular things. Find some irregular things.

Leaf cover

You need
lino tile

leaves of the same kind
scissors

Now . . .
Cut off the leaf stalks.
Fit leaves on the tile.
Cover as much of it as you can.
But make sure the leaves don't overlap.
                            don't hang over the edge.
How many leaves best cover the tile?

Funny faces

You need
polythene bag
glass bottle   plastic bottle

felt-tip pen

water

Now . . .
Draw a face on the polythene bag.
Pour water into the bag and tie the top.
Can you make the face look happy?
                          look sad?
Draw faces on the two bottles.
Will these faces change shape?

Meet a woodlouse

You need
woodlouse
hand-lens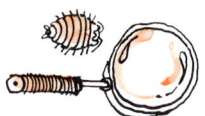

Now . . .
Look at this drawing.
Find the parts on your woodlouse.
How many <u>segments</u> can you see?
How many segments have legs?
Look carefully at the front end.
How is it different from the back end?
How do you think woodlice recognise each other?

Sound sense

You need
marble   stone
coin
tray   button
       books

Now . . .
Prop up your tray like this.
Hold each object at the top of the tray.
Describe the noise each one makes when you let it go.
Get a friend to blindfold you and choose an object
to send down the tray.
Guess what it is.

Designing wallpaper

You need

lots of small things  white kitchen paper

 paints saucer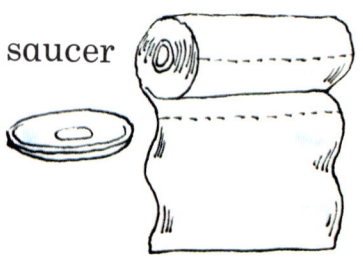

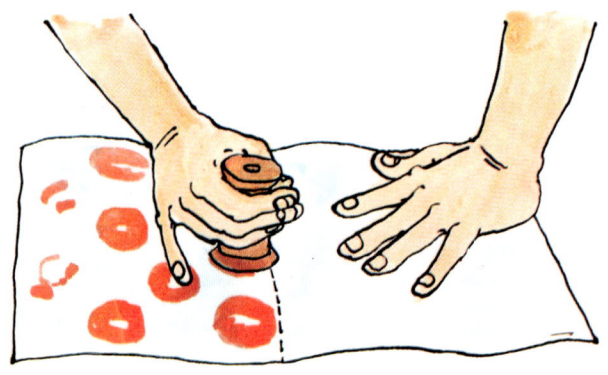

Now . . .
First, practise making prints.
Dip a cotton reel, say, into paint.
Shake off the drips.
Press the reel onto the kitchen paper.
Count to three and lift it off.
Go on until you get a clear print every time.
Try different things and different colours.
Make different designs.

Be a designer
Mrs Tessel and Mrs Random both want some new wallpaper.
Mrs Tessel likes regular things.
For example, her garden looks like this.

Mrs Random likes irregular things.
Can you find her garden?
Print a wallpaper with a
regular pattern for Mrs Tessel.
Print one that Mrs Random will like.

Little and big

How do babies change as they grow up?
Look at these pictures of babies.
Can you put them in age-order?

Jingling jars

You need

eight jars
knitting needle
jug of water
tray

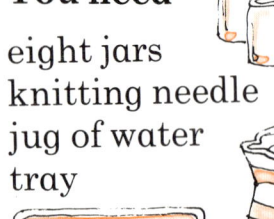

Now . . .
Put some water in a jar.
Tap the top of the jar with the needle to make a note.
Can you change the note?
(Clue: It's something to do with the water.)
Put different amounts of water in the jars
to make a set of notes.
Play a tune. Give your tune a name.

Faces

You need

round balloon
felt-tip pen

balloon pump

Now . . .
Draw a small face on your balloon.
Can you change it into a big face?
How big can you make it?
Can you make it vanish?
(Clue: Keep pumping!)

Rainbows

You need
yellow, red, blue paint

brushes

water   paper

Now . . .
Can you change your paints into new colours?
Use one of your colours
to change red to orange.
Use another to change blue to purple.
Change yellow into green.
Can you make brown?
Paint a picture with your new colours.

The last straw

You need
milk bottle top
bowl of water

drawing pins

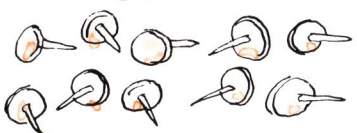

Now . . .
Float your bottle top on the water.
Load pins on board, one at a time.
What happens as you add each pin?
What happens when you add one pin too many?
Find out the meaning of the saying:
'the last straw that broke the camel's back'.

Word play

Let's change a cat into a dog.
Look: c a t
        c o t
        d o t
        d o g

Notice that one letter changes each time, to make another word.

Now turn a seed into a tree: s e e d
                            f e e d
                            f l e d
                            f l e e
                            f r e e
                            t r e e

Try changing: p i g into s t y
                h e a t into c o l d
                c o a t into h o o k
                t w o into s i x
                b u s into c a b

Invent some more word plays.

© S Parker/A Ward, 1977   Illustrated by Rowan Barnes-Murphy   Published by Thomas Nelson   Printed in Hong Kong